TEMPTING PARTY SNACKS

IMP Limited

CONTENTS

Asia & The Far East

The better organized you are beforehand, the more you and your guests will relax and enjoy the party.

WELCOMING ATMOSPHERE

Remember that your guests have come to see you, so keep the food simple so that you can greet people rather than disappearing into the kitchen. A few minutes taking hot snacks out of the oven is fine, but half an hour's frantic food arranging will leave you feeling harassed and your guests wondering whose party it is.

RUNNING SMOOTHLY

To avoid a crush, have a buffet table for food and another table for drinks. Show the snacks off to advantage by arranging them around a centre-piece: a flower arrangement, a pyramid of fruit or a large platter of crudités. Shy guests often welcome the 'prop' of handing round plates of nibbles or refilling glasses, so don't hesitate to enlist their help.

Keep alcoholic drinks simple, for instance, white and red wine, and maybe one type of beer. Mulled wine is popular at winter parties; Pimms or sangria (red wine and lemonade) in summer. Make sure you provide plentiful quantities of soft drinks, such as orange juice and sparkling water. If the theme of the party is cocktails, arrange beforehand who is going to mix them.

TOP TIPS FOR CATERING

• Provide plenty of complex carbohydrates (starch) — a large pizza cut into bite-sized pieces, garlic bread, spicy potato wedges and mini pitta breads.
• If serving a meal later, offer light titbits, such as vegetable-filled filo pastry pockets and crudités with salsa and guacamole.
• Cocktail sticks make nibbles, especially hot ones such as sausages, easier to pick up.
• Have jars of olives, nuts, packets of crisps and savoury nibbles handy in case there are extra, unexpected guests.
• Find out if anyone has special dietary needs, and keep some platefuls exclusively vegetarian.
• Enjoy the party!

GARNISH IDEAS

Cucumber flowers With a canelle knife, cut away strips of peel at 1cm/½in intervals, or make grooves with fork prongs. Slice cucumber.

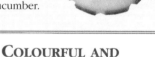

COLOURFUL AND QUICK SNACKS

Sandwiches are much more fun when cut out into stars, crescents and people. Use biscuit cutters or work freehand.

Tomato roses Cut a continuous strip, starting at base of tomato. Put peel skin-side down; roll up. Roll end loosely, like open petal.

Spring onion tassels Trim into 7.5cm/3in lengths. Make several lengthways cuts, leaving 2.5cm/1in intact root. Soak in iced water for 30 minutes.

Lemon twists Cut a lemon into slices. Cut each slice from the centre to the edge. Twist the slice into an S-shape. Make orange twists in the same way.

Contrasting crudités *(below)* Plates of raw and blanched vegetables look much more striking when grouped according to colour around a dip.

Mix and match *(left)* To cater for all your guests' tastes, include vegetables, fruit and a starchy food, such as tortilla chips. Colour contrast plate and food.

Sandwich success *(above)* Mix brown and white crustless bread triangles on the same plate. Garnish with herbs or even edible flowers, such as pansies and chives, or vegetable creations as above.

Garnishing *(right)* Herbs, olives, sesame or poppy seeds make dips such as tara-masalata, hummus and cream cheese look extra appetizing.

TOMATO AND MOZZARELLA CROSTINI

This wonderful dish has a double advantage — it is simple to make, and it reflects all the flavours of Italy. Tomato, garlic, olive oil, mozzarella and fresh basil flavours mix and mingle.

INGREDIENTS
(Makes 15 crostini)

- 15 slices plain ciabatta or French bread
- 6 tbsp olive oil
- 6 cloves garlic
- 500g/1lb 2oz ripe tomatoes
- salt and black pepper
- 200g/7oz mozzarella cheese
- pinch of cayenne pepper
- 1 bunch basil, to serve

INGREDIENTS TIP
For a piquant variation, add anchovy fillets to the crostini. Alternatively, top with a stronger cheese, such as Gorgonzola or Parmesan. Ciabatta, meaning slipper because of its shape, is the airy Italian bread made with olive oil. It is also available flavoured but, for this recipe, use plain so that the taste of the topping comes to the fore.

1 Preheat the oven to 200°C/400°F/Gas 6. Place the bread slices in an ovenproof dish and drizzle with the olive oil.

Step 1

2 Peel and finely slice the garlic. Cut each slice into slivers. Sprinkle it onto the bread. Wash the tomatoes and dry. With a small, sharp knife, cut out the green cone from the tomatoes. Slice thinly and put 2 slices on each piece of bread.

Step 2

3 Warm the bread slices in the oven for 10 minutes. Season with salt and black pepper. Dice the mozzarella cheese, add a pinch of cayenne pepper and sprinkle on top of the slices.

4 Reduce the oven temperature to 180°C/350°F/Gas 4. Return the crostini to the oven for a further 10 minutes, or until the mozzarella is melted and pale golden. Tear off the basil leaves. Serve the hot crostini garnished with basil.

Step 2

Preparation: **15** Min Cooking: **20** Min
Per Crostini: 116 kcal/483 kJ;
5g protein; 8g fat; 7g carbohydrate

TYPICALLY NEAPOLITAN
As the home of the pizza, Naples knows about inventive bread-making. Large, flat shovels are used to push the circular dough bases into huge ovens. There are many toppings and, as Naples lies on the Adriatic coastline, there is a fair chance seafood will be on the menu.

COOKING TIPS

You can prepare the crostini beforehand and heat them just before serving. In this case, do not warm the bread after adding the tomatoes. Sprinkle over the mozzarella and keep in a cool place until needed
• Use plum tomatoes in summer when they are in season, and any flavourful type at other times of year.

SERVING TIP

Serve with other Italian anti-pasti such as mortadella salami, artichokes and mixed peppers.

🍷 Serve a fresh-tasting fruity red wine, such as Valpolicella with these toasts.

COURGETTE AND CHEESE FILLED MUSHROOMS

GREECE

Your guests are bound to enjoy these mushrooms, which have plenty of flavour. A savoury filling of courgette, cheese and egg scented with oregano gives a truly Mediterranean feel.

INGREDIENTS
(Makes 20 mushrooms)

- 20 large flat mushrooms
- 3 courgettes
- 1 small onion
- 4 tbsp olive oil
- ½ tsp dried oregano
- 100g/4oz hard sheep's cheese, e.g. pecorino
- 4 eggs
- 4 tbsp milk
- salt and black pepper
- fresh oregano, to garnish

INGREDIENTS TIP
If you cannot find pecorino cheese, use a good-quality Cheddar or Emmental, or your favourite hard cheese.

1 Clean the mushrooms by wiping them with a clean cloth or kitchen paper. Remove and chop the stalks. Wash and finely dice the courgettes. Peel and dice the onion.

Step 1

2 Heat 2 tablespoons of the oil in a pan and lightly brown the mushroom caps. Remove them from the pan and place on kitchen paper to soak up excess moisture. Keep them warm on a plate at a low temperature in the oven.

3 Leave any mushroom juices that collect in the pan. Add the rest of the oil. Sauté the onion until soft. Add the courgettes and cook for 3 minutes. Add the chopped mushroom stalks and dried oregano. Simmer for 5–10 minutes, or until all the liquid evaporates.

Step 3

4 Meanwhile, roughly dice the cheese. Whisk the eggs in a bowl with the milk and season with salt and pepper. Add cheese and eggs to the courgette mixture and cook, stirring, until the eggs are set. Fill each mushroom cap with a spoonful of the mixture. Serve warm, garnished with oregano sprigs.

Step 4

Preparation: **30** Min Cooking: **15** Min
Per Mushroom: 57 kcal/236 kJ;
3g protein; 5g fat; 1g carbohydrate

TYPICALLY GREEK
The tavernas of Greece tend to be occupied by day by solitary men or card-playing groups but come to life at night. Few Greek women ever go out to tavernas but, in tourist spots, holidaymakers make up the shortfall, enjoying bazouki music to accompany their supper.

COOKING TIPS

Do not overcook the mushrooms in Step 2 as the sides need to stay firm — fry them just long enough to brown lightly and bring out the flavour • If liked, grill the filled mushrooms for a few minutes before serving to crisp up the filling.

SERVING TIP

Serve with the Greek fish roe dip taramasalata, hot pitta bread, olives, radishes and green chillies.

White wine is the best accompaniment for these snacks. Try a Sauvignon Blanc from eastern Europe.

FETA CHEESE PARCELS

GREECE

These crisp filo pastries with a savoury filling of ewes' milk cheese, scented with nutmeg and seasoned with fresh herbs, are prized in the Greek kitchen — and on the party menu.

INGREDIENTS
(Makes 25 pastries)

- 1 onion
- 1 clove garlic
- 2 tbsp olive oil
- 200g/7oz feta cheese
- black pepper
- pinch of ground nutmeg
- 3 tbsp fresh mixed herbs
- 100g/4oz butter
- 250g/9oz filo pastry

INGREDIENTS TIP

For an authentic flavour, use Greek olive oil if you can get it. Feta cheese is a soft crumbly white Greek cheese. It is matured in slices in brine (feta means slice in Greek) and is therefore salty: there is no need to add more salt to this recipe. Feta is the central ingredient of a Greek salad. Use any combination of fresh herbs, such as mint, oregano and dill.

1 Peel and finely chop the onion and garlic. Heat the oil in a pan and fry the onion and garlic for 2–3 minutes, or until softened.

2 Take the pan off the heat. Crumble the feta cheese and stir in. Season the mixture with pepper, and add the nutmeg. Chop the herbs and stir in.

Step 2

3 Preheat the oven to 180°C/350°F/Gas 4. Melt the butter in a small saucepan. Lay a sheet of pastry on the work surface and brush generously with melted butter. Cut into thirds lengthways. Meanwhile, keep the other sheets covered with a damp cloth to prevent them from drying out.

Step 3

4 Put a teaspoon of the cheese mixture into a corner of one of the pastry strips. Fold the pastry over to form a triangle. Keep folding over from side to side to form the triangular shape until you reach the end of the sheet. Seal the edges with melted butter. Repeat with rest of filling and pastry sheets.

Step 4

5 Line 2 baking sheets with greaseproof paper and place the pastries on them. Bake for 15 minutes, or until the pastries are brown and crispy. Serve hot or cold.

Preparation: **35** Min Cooking: **15** Min
Per Pastry: **88** kcal/363 kJ;
2g protein; 6g fat; 6g carbohydrate

TYPICALLY GREEK

Most Greeks still live in villages either by the sea, where fishing — and tourism — are the main sources of income, or inland as farmers. Cheese from locally reared herds of sheep and goats, home-grown vegetables and freshly caught fish are staples of the national diet.

COOKING TIPS

If liked, steam 100g/4oz of fresh spinach, chop it finely and squeeze out excess moisture. Stir into the feta filling mixture • Puff pastry works as well as filo. Roll it out and cut into squares. Fold one corner over filling onto the opposite one to form a triangle. Seal the edges. Brush with egg and bake as above.

SERVING TIP

Serve with a selection of crudités — raw vegetables cut into strips — crisprolls and black kalamata olives.

Serve these pastries with a dry white wine from Australia, such as a Semillon Chardonnay blend.

GARLIC PRAWNS WITH ALMOND DIP

SPAIN

Tiger prawns sautéed in garlic are immensely popular. Try this variation, in which the juicy prawns are arranged around a nutty almond, parsley and garlic dip.

INGREDIENTS
(Serves 10)

- 20 cooked, peeled large tiger prawns
- 5 cloves garlic
- 5 tbsp olive oil
- salt and black pepper

FOR THE DIP
- 50g/2oz ground almonds
- 250ml/9fl oz hot vegetable stock
- 1 bunch flat-leaf parsley
- 1 clove garlic
- 1 tbsp crème fraîche
- pinch of chilli powder
- 1 lemon and fresh parsley, to garnish

INGREDIENTS TIP
Buy big tiger prawns for this recipe. It is easiest to buy them already cooked and peeled but, if you want to use fresh ones, boil them for 2-3 minutes, or until they are pink, then peel them.

1 Wash and dry the prawns. Peel 5 cloves of garlic and crush into a frying pan. Add the oil and put over a medium heat. Toss the garlic for 1 minute, then add the prawns. Cook the prawns for 2 minutes, season and set aside to cool.

Step 1

2 Meanwhile, for the dip, place the ground almonds in a non-stick pan and brown them over a low heat, stirring frequently. Add the stock. Cook for 3–4 minutes, or until the mixture becomes a thick paste. Leave to cool for 5 minutes.

Step 2

3 Meanwhile, wash, dry and finely chop the parsley. Add to the almond mixture. Peel the garlic and crush it into the mixture. Fold in the crème fraîche. Season with a pinch of chilli powder, salt and pepper.

Step 3

4 Put the almond dip into a small bowl in the centre of a serving plate and arrange the prawns around it. For the garnish, wash and dry the lemon and cut into wedges. Garnish the prawns with lemon wedges and sprigs of parsley.

Preparation: **15** Min Cooking: **10** Min
Per Serving: 139 kcal/578 kJ;
11g protein; 10g fat; 2g carbohydrate

TYPICALLY ANDALUSIAN
With streets of white-washed houses, the villages of Andalusia look like many others in the Mediterranean. This area is known as the 'zona de los fritos', the zone of fried food, where pungent smells of seafood, almonds and spices linger in the warm summer air.

COOKING TIP

To serve the prawns hot, prepare the dip up to 2 days beforehand and cook the prawns at the last minute. Whisk them piping hot to the table. Do not overcook prawns or they become tough and rubbery.

SERVING TIP

Serve with a pepper-and-potato-filled Spanish omelette, Manchego cheese and serrano ham.

For a Spanish theme, serve the prawns with a glass of dry fino sherry.

SERVING TIP Serve with some wedges of lemon, crab sticks and slices of fresh crusty bread.

A crisp, zesty Chardonnay from northern Italy makes a great accompaniment.

PRAWN AND SALMON BROCHETTES

NORWAY

Made up of lemony avocado, cucumber and tiger prawns, some wrapped in smoked salmon, these kebabs are ideal summer party nibbles and, as a bonus, need no cooking.

INGREDIENTS
(Makes 6 brochettes)
- ½ cucumber
- 150g/5oz smoked salmon
- 1 avocado
- 1 lemon
- 16 cooked tiger prawns

FOR THE DIP
- 1 clove garlic
- 4 tbsp mayonnaise
- dash of Tabasco sauce
- salt and black pepper
- pinch of cayenne pepper
- salad leaves, to garnish

INGREDIENTS TIP
You can buy garlic mayonnaise rather than making your own, if wished. Tabasco sauce is made from fiery tabasco peppers, native to Mexico, vinegar and salt. A few drops are enough to flavour a dish.

1 Peel the cucumber and cut in half lengthways. Scoop out the seeds, then cut both pieces of cucumber in half lengthways again. Cut into 3cm/1½in pieces.

2 Cut salmon into strips. Peel the avocado, remove the stone and cut the flesh into 3cm/1½in pieces. Finely grate the rind and squeeze the juice from the lemon. Toss the avocado pieces in the lemon juice.

3 Wrap the salmon strips around half the cucumber pieces and prawns. Thread salmon-wrapped cucumber and prawns alternately onto 6 wooden skewers with the avocado and the remaining cucumber and prawns. Arrange skewers on a serving plate.

4 For the dip, peel the garlic and crush or finely chop. Mix with the mayonnaise. Add the Tabasco sauce and season. Spoon into a small bowl and sprinkle with cayenne pepper. Serve the brochettes straight away, garnished with salad leaves.

Step 1

Step 3

Step 4

Preparation: **20 Min**
Per Brochette: 237 kcal/987 kJ;
20g protein; 17g fat; 2g carbohydrate

TYPICALLY NORWEGIAN
The long and rocky coastline of Norway is dotted with little islands where many Norwegians have summer holiday homes. The inlets of seawater, called fjords, also make fertile ground for salmon, which is farmed to match the demand for this popular fish.

CRISP GOUDA AND HAM BALLS

THE NETHERLANDS

Dutch cheese takes on a new dimension enveloped in choux pastry with parsley and ham, and fried until crisp and light. These crunchy-coated little balls simply melt in the mouth.

INGREDIENTS

(Makes 45 balls)

- 150g/5oz Gouda cheese
- ½ bunch flat-leaf parsley
- 75g/3oz smoked ham
- 50g/2oz butter
- salt and black pepper
- pinch of paprika
- 150g/5oz plain flour
- 4 large eggs
- 1 tbsp crème fraîche
- corn, groundnut or sun- flower oil, to fry
- 1 tomato and lettuce leaves, to garnish

INGREDIENTS TIP
Experiment with different types of cheese, such as Emmental, Gruyère or Cheddar. For a vegetarian alternative, use diced peppers instead of ham.

1 Grate the cheese. Wash the parsley, dry it and chop finely. Finely dice the ham. Heat 250ml/9fl oz of water in a saucepan with the butter. Season, and add a pinch of paprika.

2 Stir until the butter has melted, but do not allow the water to boil. As soon as the butter melts and the water is about to boil, quickly beat in the flour until it forms a soft, smooth paste. Cook for 2 minutes, stirring constantly. Leave to cool slightly.

Step 2

3 Put the mixture in a bowl and whisk in the eggs one by one. Do not let the mixture become too runny. Mix in the cheese, ham, parsley and crème fraîche.

Step 4

4 Heat the oil in a deep-fat fryer to 180°C/350°F or until a cube of white bread takes 1 minute to turn brown. Drop spoon-fuls of mixture into the oil, 8–10 at a time, and fry for 5 minutes, or until golden brown.

5 Remove the balls from the oil and drain them on kitchen paper. Cut the tomato into wedges. Serve the balls hot or cold, with tomato wedges on a bed of lettuce.

Step 5

Preparation: 30 Min Cooking: 30 Min
Per Ball: 50 kcal/207 kJ;
2g protein; 4g fat; 3g carbohydrate

TYPICALLY DUTCH
Windmills are part of the flat, lush landscape of Holland, and you can even find biscuits called *speculaas* in the shape of windmills. They are flavoured with oriental spices such as cardamom, a legacy of Holland's exotic trading links dating back to the 16th century.

COOKING TIPS

If you do not have a deep-fat fryer or wish to avoid cooking with oil, bake the balls in an oven preheated to 200°C/400°F/Gas 6. Place teaspoonfuls of mixture on a greased baking sheet. Bake for 25 minutes, or until they are risen and golden brown • Serve with cocktail sticks so the balls are easier to pick up.

SERVING TIP

Serve a selection of Dutch cheeses, radishes and tomatoes with some crusty rye bread.

To drink, offer your guests ice-cold Dutch beer or a glass of Genever (Dutch gin).

DEEP-FRIED MUSHROOMS

AUSTRIA

A golden breadcrumb coating transforms the modest mushroom into a delicious appetizer. Serve it with a tangy rémoulade — mayonnaise flavoured with gherkins, capers and mustard.

INGREDIENTS

(Serves 4)

- 500g/1lb 2oz button mushrooms
- 4 tbsp plain flour
- salt and pepper
- pinch of paprika
- 2 eggs
- 90g/3½oz white breadcrumbs

FOR THE REMOULADE

- 1 bunch flat-leaf parsley
- 1 small onion
- 2 small gherkins
- 2 tsp capers
- 100g/4oz mayonnaise
- 100g/4oz natural yoghurt
- 2 tsp lemon juice
- 2 tsp mild mustard
- corn or sunflower oil, to fry
- lemon wedges, to garnish

INGREDIENTS TIP

You can buy dried bread-crumbs in supermarkets, but making your own is a good way to use up stale bread.

1 Clean the mushrooms with a soft brush. Season the flour with salt, pepper and a pinch of paprika and put in a shallow bowl. Whisk the eggs lightly and pour into another bowl. Put the breadcrumbs into a third bowl.

2 For the rémoulade, wash and dry the parsley. Chop it finely. Peel and dice the onion. Dice the gherkins. Roughly chop the capers. Mix all these with the mayonnaise and yoghurt. Add the lemon juice and mustard and season with salt and pepper. Leave in a cool place until required.

3 Heat the oil in a heavy-based pan, until a cube of white bread takes 1 minute to turn brown, or in a deep-fat fryer to 180°C/350°F. Make sure that the oil level is well below the top of the pan.

4 Coat each mushroom in flour, then egg and finally the breadcrumbs. Make sure that each mushroom is thoroughly coated. Fry the mushrooms in batches 8–10 at a time for 6 minutes, or until golden brown. Drain them on kitchen paper. Serve the mushrooms hot, garnished with lemon wedges and the rémoulade on the side.

Step 2

Step 4

Step 4

Preparation: 30 Min Cooking: 30 Min
Per Serving: 535 kcal/2228 kJ;
12g protein; 39g fat; 38g carbohydrate

TYPICALLY AUSTRIAN

There's nothing like an energetic day in the mountains of the Tyrol to whet the appetite for Gustostückerln (titbits) from the melting pot of Austria's culinary heritage. Tyrolean Schlutz pastries are a favourite, filled with mince, curd cheese or spinach.

COOKING TIP

You can shallow-fry the mushrooms if you prefer. Heat
5 tablespoonfuls of oil in a deep frying pan. Cook the
mushrooms for 8–10 minutes, turning frequently, until
they are golden brown. Remove them with a slotted
spoon and drain on kitchen paper before serving.

SERVING TIP

Serve with rye bread spread
with a coarse country-style pâté,
garnished with lettuce and lemon.

Try a warming cup of jagertee — hot black tea
with Austrian rum — or a dark beer.

ONION AND BACON PRETZELS

GERMANY

Hand round these fresh soft pretzels, flavoured with onions, bacon and coriander, at a party and watch them go. Like bread rolls, they also make a good accompaniment to any meal.

INGREDIENTS
(Makes 16 pretzels)

- 500g/1lb 2oz strong white bread flour
- 1 sachet (7g/¼oz) easy-blend dried yeast
- 1 tsp caster sugar
- 1 tsp ground coriander
- 1 tsp salt
- 1 egg
- 1 large onion
- 150g/5oz smoked, rindless bacon
- 2 tbsp vegetable oil
- milk, to glaze
- coarse sea salt, to sprinkle

INGREDIENTS TIP
For vegetarians, leave out the bacon and instead add 100g/4oz of chopped olives or sun-dried tomatoes at Step 3. For a true Bavarian flavour, add 2 tablespoons of caraway seeds.

1 Put the flour, yeast, sugar, coriander and salt into a bowl. Make a well in the centre and add the egg and 250ml/9fl oz water. Mix thoroughly to form a soft dough, adding more water if necessary. Knead the dough on a lightly floured board for 5 minutes.

2 Place the dough back in the bowl. Cover with a tea towel. Leave to rise in a warm place for 45 minutes, or until doubled in size.

3 Meanwhile, peel and chop the onion. Finely dice the bacon. Heat the oil in a pan. Add the onion and bacon and fry gently until the onion is soft but not brown. Cool. Once the dough has risen, add the onion and bacon. Knead again to incorporate.

4 Preheat the oven to 200°C/400°F/Gas 6. Line a baking sheet with greaseproof paper. Divide the dough into 16 equal portions. Roll out each one between your hands into a long, thin strip. Cross each strip over into a pretzel shape. Leave to rise again for 20 minutes in a warm place.

5 Brush the pretzels with milk. Sprinkle them with coarse sea salt. Bake for 25 minutes, or until golden brown.

Step 1

Step 3

Step 4

Preparation: 30 Min
Rising: 1 Hour 5 Min
Cooking: 25 Min
Per Pretzel: 151 kcal/637 kJ;
6g protein; 4g fat; 25g carbohydrate

TYPICALLY BAVARIAN
The cereal belt around Munich provides the raw materials both for Bavaria's renowned beer and for its bread and pretzels. At the Oktoberfest — Munich's yearly beer festival — ale-drinkers come out in force, and locals and tourists alike enjoy a tankard or two.

COOKING TIP

The pretzels are best served warm and fresh. But if you have some left over or you wish to make them ahead of time, freeze them on the day of baking, wrapped in a polythene bag. To serve, defrost, then heat through in an oven preheated to 180°C/350°F/Gas 4 for 10 minutes.

SERVING TIP

Serve the pretzels with a grilled German Bratwurst sausage, sauerkraut (pickled cabbage) and mustard.

A Californian Zinfandel red wine balances these savoury pretzels perfectly.

$\mathscr{M}$INI QUICHES LORRAINES

NORTHERN FRANCE

These miniature versions of the classic French quiche make perfect party food. Alternatively, make them up as part of a picnic for those long, hot days of summer.

INGREDIENTS

(Makes 10 quiches)

- 175g/6oz plain flour
- salt and black pepper
- 80g/3¼oz butter

FOR THE FILLING

- 90g/3½oz smoked ham
- 90g/3½oz roast ham
- 100g/4oz Gruyère cheese
- pinch each of paprika and nutmeg
- 142ml/5fl oz double cream
- 3 eggs

INGREDIENTS TIP
You can use bacon as an alternative to the ham. Dice it and sauté lightly for a few minutes before mixing with the other filling ingredients. If wished, replace the Gruyère with Cheddar or any other medium-hard cheese. To speed up the preparation, buy shortcrust pastry instead of making it.

1 Mix the flour with salt and black pepper. Cut the butter into pieces and rub in with 3–4 tablespoons of cold water, enough to form a soft dough. Wrap the dough in non-PVC cling film and chill for 1 hour.

2 For the filling, dice the hams and grate the cheese. Preheat the oven to 180°C/350°F/Gas 4. Grease 10 small fluted tartlet tins, about 8cm/3¼in in diameter.

3 Roll the pastry into a log and cut it into 10 equal portions. Roll each portion into a 10cm/4in round.

4 Line the tins with the pastry, pushing it well into the corners without stretching it. Cut off any overhanging pieces of pastry.

5 Sprinkle the ham and cheese evenly into the pastry cases. Sprinkle over the paprika and nutmeg. Whisk the cream with the eggs and season with salt and pepper. Pour the egg mixture into each of the pastry cases, not quite to the top.

6 Bake the quiches for 20–25 minutes, or until they are golden brown and the filling is set. Serve immediately.

Step 3

Step 4

Step 5

Preparation: **1** Hour Chilling: **1** Hour
Cooking: **25** Min
Per Quiche: 269 kcal/1117 kJ;
10g protein; 19g fat; 14g carbohydrate

TYPICALLY LORRAINE
Like timber-boarded houses, the origins of the Quiche Lorraine go back to the 16th century. It was invented in Nancy in the heart of the region, and is still the town's speciality, called *féouse* locally. To start with a bread dough was used, but nowadays it is pastry based.

COOKING TIPS

Pastry ends up lighter and is easier to make if the ingredients, especially the butter, are cold • Put the tartlet tins on a baking tray so they are easier to transfer to and from the oven • If you do not have tartlet tins, make one quiche to fit a 30cm/12in round tin and serve in slices. Fill and bake for 25–30 minutes.

SERVING TIP

Serve the quiches Lorraines with steamed asparagus spears and hollandaise sauce.

A country red wine such as Cabernet Sauvignon Vin de Pays d'Oc is ideal with these quiches.

SERVING TIP Serve with other savoury snacks such as cheese straws, filled tartlets or mini Welsh rarebits.

The sweet and spicy flavours go perfectly with a glass of Martini Brut, the Italian sparkling wine.

DEVILS ON HORSEBACK

GREAT BRITAIN

INGREDIENTS
(Makes 40 savouries)
- 40 whole almonds
- 20 no-need-to-soak dried apricots
- 20 stoned prunes
- 20 rashers of smoked rindless streaky bacon
- black pepper
- 2 tbsp olive oil, to grill
- flat-leaf parsley, to garnish

INGREDIENTS TIP
Use the 'ready to eat' prunes and apricots as these are the juiciest. Alternatively, buy organic varieties, free of additives and preservatives, which are available in health food shops. To cut down on preparation time in Step 1, you can use blanched, ready-peeled almonds.

This is a simple dish to prepare but the contrasting ingredients provide a taste sensation in the mouth. Served on cocktail sticks, the bite-sized portions make the perfect party nibble.

1 Put the almonds into a bowl and cover them in boiling water. Leave to stand for 10 minutes, then peel off the skin. Stuff one almond into each apricot and prune.

2 Stretch the bacon rashers with the back of a knife to prevent them from shrinking during cooking. Chop each one in half.

3 Roll each prune and each apricot in half a rasher. Season with pepper. Lay out on a baking tray and brush with oil. Preheat the grill to medium-high.

4 Grill the devils on horseback for 10 minutes, turning to brown all over, until the bacon is crisp. Serve immediately, garnished with sprigs of parsley.

Step 1

Step 2

Step 3

Preparation: **20** Min Standing: **10** Min
Grilling: **10** Min
Per Savoury: **61** kcal/256 kJ;
2g protein; 4g fat; 4g carbohydrate

TYPICALLY ENGLISH
Devils on horseback started life as a savoury, eaten at dinner after the dessert to cleanse the palate before the gentlemen embarked on a port-drinking session. Nowadays, savoury titbits are served at all sorts of festivities, from cocktail parties to nostalgic maypole dances.

$\mathscr{S}$MOKED SALMON PARTY BITES

GREAT BRITAIN

For a special occasion, offer these elegant snacks: smoked salmon and fresh cream, flavoured with dill and blended to a buttery paste, then spread on crisp slices of French bread.

INGREDIENTS

(Makes 20 bites)

- 4 sheets leaf gelatine
- 1 unwaxed lemon
- 1 bunch dill
- 250g/9oz smoked salmon
- 2 tbsp crème fraîche
- 90ml/3fl oz double cream
- salt and white pepper
- ½ tsp paprika
- 20 slices French bread
- 50g/2oz cream cheese
- slices of lemon, to garnish
- rocket leaves and edible flowers, e.g. pansies or nasturtiums, to garnish, optional

INGREDIENTS TIP

You can use smoked salmon trimmings in this recipe, which are less expensive than whole slices. As an alternative, try smoked halibut or mackerel.

1 Soak the gelatine leaves in cold water for 5 minutes. Wash and dry the lemon. Grate the rind and squeeze the juice. Wash and dry the dill. Reserve a few sprigs for garnish and finely chop the rest.

2 Place the smoked salmon and crème fraîche in a food processor and blend to a fine paste. Mix in the dill. Warm 250ml/9fl oz of water in a pan. Squeeze the excess water out of the gelatine leaves and dissolve them in the warm water. Mix the gelatine into the salmon paste a spoonful at a time.

3 Whip the cream lightly and fold into the salmon mixture, together with the lemon rind and juice. Season the mousse with salt, white pepper and paprika and leave to set for 1 hour in the fridge.

4 Preheat the grill to high. Toast the bread slices until golden and crisp. Spread a little cream cheese on each slice.

5 Spoon the mousse into a piping bag fitted with a large star nozzle. Pipe a generous swirl of mousse onto each slice of bread. Serve garnished with dill and triangles of lemon, and with rocket and flowers, if using.

Step 2

Step 3

Step 5

Preparation: **30** Min Setting: **1** Hour
Per Bite: 103 kcal/431 kJ
6g protein; 5g fat; 9g carbohydrate

TYPICALLY SCOTTISH

Fishing in rivers and lochs has long been a necessity for highland crofters and a passion with the aristocracy. Smoked salmon was traditionally created by hanging the fish in the chimney over the ever-burning peat fire, but now it is big, mechanized business.

COOKING TIP

When using gelatine, do not let the water get too hot. Overheating makes it go stringy and the mousse may not set. Aim for hand-warm water, then take the pan off the heat to add the gelatine. Return it to the heat only if the gelatine does not dissolve.

SERVING TIP

Accompany with crudités (sliced raw vegetables) and a Greek yoghurt, onion and chive dip.

 Champagne or sparkling wine is the perfect accompaniment for these luxury canapés.

$\mathscr{S}$PICED BEAN NUGGETS

You can prepare these bite-sized balls in advance, so there is no need for last-minute party panics. Simply shape, cover and chill the nuggets until you are ready to deep-fry them.

INGREDIENTS
(Makes 24 nuggets)

- 225g/8oz dried black-eyed beans
- 1 onion
- 1 red chilli
- ½ bunch spring onions
- 1 large egg
- salt and black pepper
- sunflower oil, to deep-fry

INGREDIENTS TIP
Black-eyed beans are small and creamy in taste and appearance, with an attractive black mark where they joined the pod. They are delicious in curries and bean cakes, often served with rice. You can vary the beans for this recipe. Try, for instance, chick-peas or cannellini beans (also sold as Italian haricot beans or white kidney beans).

1 Put the beans in a bowl and cover with cold water. Leave to soak overnight. Drain the beans and put in a pan with plenty of cold water. Bring to the boil, then boil rapidly for 10 minutes. Reduce heat and simmer for 20 minutes, or until tender. Drain and rinse under cold running water.

2 Peel and roughly chop the onion. Put the beans and onion in a food processor and blend until they form a smooth paste.

3 Wearing rubber gloves, de-seed and finely chop the chilli. Chop the spring onions. Mix into the bean and onion paste, together with the egg and seasoning. Shape the mixture into 24 even-sized balls.

4 Heat the oil in a deep-fat fryer to 180°C/350°F, or in a deep saucepan until a cube of white bread takes 1 minute to turn brown. Cook the nuggets in batches for 1–2 minutes, or until golden and heated through. Drain on kitchen paper and serve warm, straight away.

Step 1

Step 3

Step 4

Soaking: **12** Hours
Preparation: **25** Min Cooking: **40** Min
Per Nugget: **54** kcal/226 kJ;
3g protein; 3g fat; 6g carbohydrate

TYPICALLY EGYPTIAN
Traditional recipes are as old as camel rides to the sun-baked pyramids. In the desert, the aroma of beans dressed simply with garlic, oil and lemon is likely to stir your hunger pangs from morning until night, as the dish is eaten for breakfast as well as dinner.

COOKING TIPS

Make sure that you boil the beans hard and fast, uncovered, for 10 minutes to kill off toxic substances present that can be harmful to health • Do not add salt to the beans during cooking as this toughens the skins • Take care not to deep-fry the balls for longer than the specified cooking time or they disintegrate.

SERVING TIP

Follow with a typical Arabian dessert: stewed apricots with almond-flavoured rice and liqueur.

A Sicilian red wine will go well with the heat of the chilli in these spicy nibbles.

3 WAYS WITH MINI PIZZAS

These tiny pizzas provide a culinary journey through the flavours of Italy. You can guarantee that they will go down a treat at parties.

BASIC PIZZA DOUGH

Preparation: **15** Min   Rising: **45** Min

(MAKES 20 PIZZAS)
- 300g/10½oz strong white bread flour
- 1 tbsp salt
- 1 sachet (7g/¼oz) easy-blend dried yeast
- 2 tbsp olive oil
- 150ml/¼ pint luke-warm water

1 Mix flour, salt and yeast in a bowl. Make a well in the centre and add oil and half water.

2 Draw in the liquid, adding enough water to form a very soft dough. Knead dough for 5 minutes. Cover; let rise in a warm place for 45 minutes.

3 Preheat the oven to 230°C/450°F/Gas 8. Lightly grease a baking sheet with oil. Knead the dough again and divide into 20 pieces. Roll each one out on a lightly floured board to a 10–7.5cm/4–3in round and place on the sheet. Finish off with one of the 3 toppings below.

MINI PIZZAS WITH GORGONZOLA

Preparation: **10** Min   Cooking: **10–15** Min

LOMBARDY

- 200g/7oz tomato purée
- salt and black pepper
- 2 tsp dried thyme
- 125g/4½oz button mushrooms
- 200g/7oz Gorgonzola cheese
- 125g/4½oz mozzarella cheese

4 Season the tomato purée and mix in the thyme. Spread over the pizza bases.

5 Slice the mushrooms and put on top of the purée. Finely dice the cheeses and sprinkle evenly over the pizzas.

6 Bake the mini pizzas in the oven for 10–15 minutes, or until the edges are crisp.

MINI PIZZAS WITH HERBS

Preparation: **10** Min Cooking: **10–15** Min

GENOA

- 125g/4½oz mozzarella cheese
- 4 tomatoes
- salt and black pepper
- 3 bunches fresh Mediterranean herbs, e.g. basil, parsley, oregano, thyme
- 50g/2oz pine nuts
- 100ml/3½fl oz olive oil

4 Slice the mozzarella cheese and tomatoes and place them on the pizza bases. Season.

5 Finely chop the herbs. Sprinkle on top of the cheese and tomato. Roughly chop the pine nuts and sprinkle over. Drizzle the pizzas with olive oil.

6 Bake in the oven for 10–15 minutes, or until the pizzas are light brown and crisp.

MINI PIZZAS WITH TOMATO AND MOZZARELLA

Preparation: **10** Min Cooking: **10–15** Min

NAPLES

- 250g/9oz mozzarella cheese
- 300g/10½oz cherry tomatoes
- salt and black pepper
- 100ml/3½fl oz olive oil
- 1 bunch basil

4 Cut the mozzarella cheese into thin slices and divide it between the pizza bases. Cut the tomatoes in half. Place cut side down on top of the cheese.

5 Sprinkle with salt and pepper and drizzle over the olive oil.

6 Bake in the oven for 10–15 minutes. Tear the basil leaves. Serve the mini pizzas garnished with basil.

MEATBALLS IN SATAY SAUCE

THAILAND

These spicy pork balls are delicately flavoured in true Thai style, and served with a crunchy peanut dip. Guests will enjoy the winning combination of familiar and unusual ingredients.

INGREDIENTS

(Makes 30 meatballs)

- 2 spring onions
- 2 cloves garlic
- 100g/4oz canned water chestnuts
- 6 sprigs fresh coriander
- 300g/10½oz minced pork
- 2 tbsp light soy sauce
- ½ tsp caster sugar
- black pepper
- 2 tbsp groundnut oil, to fry

FOR THE DIP

- 3 tbsp smooth peanut butter
- 5 tbsp dry sherry or rice wine
- 5 tbsp light soy sauce
- 1 tbsp sambal oelek or hot chilli sauce
- 2 tbsp roasted peanuts, to garnish
- spring onions, cucumber and chillies, to garnish

1 Wash the spring onions, discard the outer layers and chop the onions into fine rings. Peel and chop the garlic. Drain the water chestnuts and dice them finely. Wash and chop the coriander.

2 Put the minced pork into a bowl and mix it with 2 tablespoons of soy sauce and the sugar. Add the onions, garlic, coriander and water chestnuts. Season with pepper and leave to stand for 30 minutes in a cool place.

3 For the dip, whisk together the peanut butter, sherry or rice wine, soy sauce and the sambal oelek or hot chilli sauce with 2 tablespoons of water until well blended. Season with black pepper.

4 Roll the pork mixture into walnut-sized balls. Heat the oil in a frying pan and fry the balls for 15–20 minutes, turning them frequently, until they are evenly browned.

5 Drain the balls on kitchen paper to absorb excess oil. Sprinkle roast peanuts over the dip and serve it with the meatballs, garnished with chillies, cucumber slices and spring onion bundles (see Cooking Tips).

Step 1

Step 4

Step 5

Preparation: **45** Min Standing: **30** Min
Cooking: **15–20** Min
Per Meatball: 55 kcal/227 kJ;
3g protein; 4g fat; 1g carbohydrate

TYPICALLY THAI

Crunchy-textured water chestnuts are much used in Thai appetizers and in sweet dishes. In Britain they are sold in cans in the super-market but in Thailand you can buy them fresh with their dark brown skins on or peeled in water in plastic bags.

COOKING TIPS

For chilli flowers, wear rubber gloves. Slice the end off a small chilli and scoop out the seeds. Cut the chilli into strips lengthways, about 1cm/½in from the stalk, keeping the stalk end intact. Soak in cold water until required • For spring onion bundles, tie equal-length strips of spring onion with a strip of red chilli.

SERVING TIP

Serve with deep-fried spring rolls filled with tiger prawns flavoured with lemon and coriander.

Offer a glass of cold beer, such as Singha, or an exotic fruit punch.

SERVING TIP Serve on a bed of lettuce with a dip of light soy sauce, lime juice, crushed garlic and sugar.

A white wine, such as an Australian Chardonnay, makes a terrific combination with these snacks.

CHICKEN SPRING ROLLS

THAILAND

For this light and crispy party snack, tender chicken morsels and crunchy beansprouts are flavoured with fresh ginger and garlic. Impress your guests with your oriental expertise.

INGREDIENTS

(Makes 16 spring rolls)

- 16 medium-sized spring roll wrappers
- 5cm/2in piece root ginger
- 250g/9oz skinless, boneless chicken breasts
- 200g/7oz beansprouts
- 3 tbsp groundnut oil
- 1 tbsp soy sauce
- black pepper
- 2 tsp garlic purée
- corn, groundnut or sun-flower oil, to deep-fry

INGREDIENTS TIP

You can buy spring roll wrappers, usually frozen, from Asian supermarkets. For this recipe use medium size, about 22cm/8½in square. Garlic purée comes in jars or tubes. To make it, put 2-3 cloves of garlic and a teaspoon of coarse sea salt in a pestle in a mortar. Crush to a fine paste.

1 If the wrappers are frozen, leave at room temperature for 30 minutes. Peel and finely shred the ginger. Wash and dry the chicken breasts and dice them finely. Rinse and drain the beansprouts.

2 Heat 3 tablespoons of oil in a pan. Add the ginger and chicken and brown for a few minutes. Add the soy sauce, pepper, garlic purée and beansprouts and stir thoroughly. Remove from the heat and leave the mixture to cool.

Step 2

3 Take a wrapper. Place a spoonful of the chicken mixture at one end. Fold in both sides and brush the surface with water. Roll up the filling into the pastry, again brushing the end with water to secure it. Leave the roll to one side and repeat the procedure with the remaining filling and wrappers.

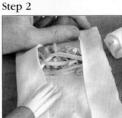

Step 3

4 Heat the oil in a deep-fat fryer or heavy-based saucepan to 180°C/350°F, or until a cube of white bread takes 1 minute to turn brown. Fry the spring rolls, 4–6 at a time, until they are light golden brown and crisp. Drain them on kitchen paper and serve hot.

Step 4

Preparation: 30 Min Cooking: 20 Min
Per Spring Roll: 111 kcal/463 kJ;
5g protein; 7g fat; 8g carbohydrate

TYPICALLY THAI

Fast food takes on a new dimension in Thailand. In cities such as Bangkok many people eat their meals from street stalls. Delicious and wholesome dishes are cooked in front of you, tailor made to your order, at a fraction of the expense of a restaurant dinner.

KOREAN POTATO FRITTERS

KOREA

INGREDIENTS

(Makes 16 fritters)

- 1 large onion
- 500g/1lb 2oz potatoes
- 3 spring onions
- 2 eggs
- 3 tbsp cornflour
- salt and black pepper
- vegetable oil, to fry

FOR THE DIP

- 2 cloves garlic
- 2 tsp sesame seeds
- 1 small red chilli
- 60ml/2fl oz light soy sauce
- 1 tbsp sake
- 1 tbsp sesame oil
- 2 tsp caster sugar

INGREDIENTS TIP

Use any potato variety.
You can use sherry instead
of sake, a rice wine.
Substitute any nutty oil, such
as walnut, for sesame oil.

Impress your guests with this Asian version of little potato patties. In Korea, the fritters are traditionally served with a punchy soy and sesame dip, as here, to give the snack a kick.

1 Peel and grate the onion and potatoes. Put the potatoes on a clean tea towel and wring out the excess moisture. Mix with the onion. Slice 1 spring onion and stir in.

2 Whisk the eggs with the cornflour. Add salt and black pepper. Combine the egg mixture with the potato and onion.

3 For the dip, peel and finely chop the garlic and remaining 2 spring onions. Toast the sesame seeds under a hot grill. Wearing rubber gloves, de-seed the chilli and dice finely. Mix all the dip ingredients and put in a serving bowl.

4 Heat a little vegetable oil in a frying pan. Drop two or three ½ tablespoonfuls of the potato mixture into it. Flatten with a spatula and fry on both sides until crisp and brown. Repeat with all of the potato mixture. Serve the fritters hot with the dipping sauce.

Step 1

Step 1

Step 4

Preparation: **25** Min Cooking: **30** Min
Per Fritter: 95 kcal/396 kJ;
2g protein; 5g fat; 11g carbohydrate

TYPICALLY KOREAN

Every year, Koreans celebrate the origins of their country. According to legend, a bear turned into a woman, using a spell involving 20 cloves of garlic. The bear-woman had a son called Tan'gun by a god, represented by a bull. Tan'gun went on to found Korea.

COOKING TIPS

Once each fritter is cooked, put it onto some kitchen paper to absorb any excess oil, then keep it warm in the oven • For a party, you can make the fritters beforehand and, just before serving, heat them in a medium oven until crisp • If wished, toast the sesame seeds in a dry frying pan instead of grilling them.

SERVING TIP

Serve with another Korean dish: marinated, skewered beef with dips and a beansprout and pepper salad.

A rich, rounded white wine is best with this dish. Try a Semillon from Australia.

CRISPY VEGETABLE WONTONS

CHINA

Few of your guests will be able to resist these golden bites. The vegetarian pastries are perfect to hand round at a party, or serve them as part of a buffet with a chilli sauce to dip them in.

INGREDIENTS

(Makes 18 wontons)

- 1 tbsp sunflower oil
- 1 clove garlic
- ½ small onion
- 50g/2oz oyster mushrooms
- 1 tbsp soy sauce
- ½ red pepper
- 100g/4oz baby sweetcorn
- 50g/2oz canned bamboo shoots
- fresh coriander
- vegetable oil, to deep-fry
- 18 x 9cm/3½in square wonton skins
- 1 egg
- chilli sauce, to dip, optional

INGREDIENTS TIP
Fresh or frozen wonton skins are available from oriental food stores or larger supermarkets. Alternatively, you can use sheets of ready-made filo pastry. Use flat or button instead of oyster mushrooms, if wished.

1 Heat the sunflower oil in a wok or frying pan. Peel and chop the garlic and onion and add. Cook for 2 minutes, stirring. Finely slice the mushrooms and add with the soy sauce. Stir-fry for 1 minute, or until the mushrooms start to wilt.

2 De-seed and finely chop the pepper and slice the sweetcorn. Add and stir-fry for 2 minutes. Drain and roughly chop the bamboo shoots. Chop 2 tablespoons of coriander. Stir both in.

3 Heat vegetable oil in a deep-fat fryer or pan to 180°C/350°F. While it heats up, divide the vegetable mix equally between the wonton skins. Beat the egg and use to brush the edges of the pastry. Bring the edges of the wontons together and press to seal, enclosing the filling.

4 Deep-fry the filled wontons in batches for 2–3 minutes, or until golden brown. Drain on kitchen paper. Keep warm while frying remaining batches. Serve hot, with a dip of chilli sauce, if wished.

Step 2

Step 3

Step 4

Preparation: **20 Min** Cooking: **10 Min**
Per Wonton: 57 kcal/237 kJ;
1g protein; 3g fat; 6g carbohydrate

TYPICALLY CHINESE
Vegetables are pivotal in Chinese cooking because meat is expensive and can be limited by religion. Nevertheless, Cantonese dishes may include such bizarre ingredients as rice worms from the paddy fields, birds' nests, snakes and even some dogs!

COOKING TIP

Test the heat of the deep-fat fryer or pan by tossing a cube of white bread into the oil. It should brown in 1 minute. Frying in batches can bring the temperature of the oil down, so check that it is hot enough in between. If the oil is not hot enough, the wontons will be greasy and limp instead of crisp and dry.

SERVING TIP

Follow with toffee apples: dip apple slices in batter, deep-fry, coat in toffee and sprinkle with sesame seeds.

Try a glass of chilled rosado red wine from Navarra in northern Spain with these snacks.

SERVING TIP Serve with a chilli dipping sauce, and give your guests the option of using chopsticks.

A glass of chilled Chinese beer or a chilled rosé from Provence complements the crunchy toasts.

𝒮ESAME PRAWN TOASTS

CHINA

INGREDIENTS
(Serves 4)

- 25g/1oz butter
- 175g/6oz cooked, peeled prawns (thawed if frozen)
- sea salt
- 1 tbsp cornflour
- 1 egg white
- 4 slices thin-cut white bread
- 75g/3oz sesame seeds
- sunflower oil, to fry

INGREDIENTS TIP
Sea salt is the result of evaporating sea water and comes in fine grains or crystals. It does not contain the additives that make table salt flow freely. Sesame seeds can be brown, red, black or, most often, sand coloured. They have a nutty flavour and are suitable for sweet and savoury dishes. Store in an airtight jar in a cool dark place. You can also freeze them for up to a year.

These crisp, buttery prawn toasts, flavoured with sesame, make an authentic party titbit, or a starter for a dinner party. They are as quick and easy to make as they are to eat.

1 Melt the butter. Using a fork, mash together the butter and prawns in a large bowl. Add some salt and the cornflour. Lightly beat the egg white and stir in.

2 Divide the prawn mixture between the slices of bread and spread evenly. Cut the crusts off the bread and discard.

3 Sprinkle sesame seeds thickly over the prawn mixture and press down. Cut the bread into 3 rectangles per slice.

4 Fill a wok or deep frying pan with oil about 2.5cm/1in deep. Heat until almost smoking. Cook the bread in batches for 2 minutes, turning once, until golden.

5 Using a slotted spoon, remove the toasts from the wok or pan. Drain them on kitchen paper. Keep warm while cooking the remaining toasts. Serve hot.

Step 1

Step 2

Step 3

Preparation: **15** Min Cooking: **6** Min
Per Serving: **450** kcal/1870 kJ;
17g protein; 34g fat; 20g carbohydrate

TYPICALLY CHINESE
People celebrate Chinese New Year in style, dressing up in dragon costumes, dancing and letting off firecrackers. Street vendors in cities such as Shanghai and Beijing do a roaring trade, serving snacks straight from the wok to the enthusiastic revellers and performers.

Asia & The Far East **41**

$\mathcal{S}$PICY CHICKEN KEBABS

INDONESIA

Grill marinated chicken on skewers and serve hot with a honey-chilli dip. The kebabs are easy for your guests to eat with their fingers, and you can cook them on the barbecue in summer.

INGREDIENTS
(Makes 16 kebabs)

- 700g/1½lb skinless, boneless chicken breasts

FOR THE MARINADE
- 1 clove garlic
- 6 tbsp groundnut oil
- 5 tbsp ketjap manis
- black pepper

FOR THE DIP
- 2 small red chillies
- 1 onion
- 1 clove garlic
- 2 tbsp groundnut oil
- 150ml/¼ pint chicken stock
- 1 tbsp cornflour
- 4 tbsp soy sauce
- 4 tbsp honey

INGREDIENTS TIP
Ketjap manis is a seasoning from Indonesia found in large supermarkets and Asian shops. You can use soy sauce instead, sweetened with 2 teaspoons of sugar.

1 Wash and pat dry the chicken breasts and cut them into 2cm/¾in cubes. For the marinade, peel and chop the garlic and mix it with the oil, ketjap manis and pepper. Place the chicken cubes in a bowl and top with the marinade. Leave for at least 2 hours in a cool place, or overnight in the fridge.

2 For the dip, halve the chillies, remove the stalks and seeds and chop them finely. Wash your hands thoroughly afterwards.

3 Peel and finely dice the onion and garlic. Heat the oil in a pan and lightly brown the onion and garlic. Add the chillies and stock and simmer for 2 minutes.

4 Mix the cornflour to a paste with 1 table-spoon of water. Add it to the pan, stirring constantly, until the mixture thickens. Add the soy sauce and honey and simmer for 3 minutes. Leave to cool.

5 Preheat the grill to high. Thread 4 cubes of chicken onto each skewer. Lay them on a grill pan in a single layer. Pour over the remaining marinade. Grill them for 10–15 minutes, turning frequently, until golden brown. Serve the kebabs hot with the dip.

Step 1

Step 2

Step 5

Preparation: **45** Min
Marinating: **2** Hours
Cooking: **10–15** Min
Per Kebab: 103 kcal/433 kJ;
11g protein; 4g fat; 6g carbohydrate

TYPICALLY INDONESIAN
Since Indonesia is made up of a mass of islands, with villages separated by lush forest and mountains, regional, religious and ethnic customs remain distinct. Processions and dances, shadow plays and funeral rites are enacted today much as in ancestral times.

COOKING TIPS

Soak wooden skewers in cold water for 10 minutes before using to stop them burning • The chicken is cooked when the juices run clear, not pink • You could serve a satay sauce made from equal parts coconut cream and peanut butter, with soy sauce, chillies, lemon juice, fresh ginger and garlic to taste.

SERVING TIP

Serve these kebabs as part of a party spread with sesame prawn toasts and a spicy dip.

🍷 White wine, such as Californian Chardonnay, combines beautifully with the honey glaze.

VEGETABLE PAKORAS WITH MANGO CHUTNEY

INDIA

From the land of the maharajas, enjoy mixed vegetables fried in an exotic batter and served with home-made chutney. These little delicacies will thrill your guests.

INGREDIENTS
(Makes 30 pakoras)

- 200g/7oz gram flour
- ½ tsp each of turmeric, cayenne pepper, garam masala and ground cumin
- 1 tsp salt
- 2 each of carrots, potatoes and small onions
- fresh parsley

FOR THE CHUTNEY

- 1 onion
- 1 mango
- 2-3 small red chillies
- 1 tsp ghee or vegetable oil
- 125ml/4fl oz vegetable stock
- 50g/2oz caster sugar
- ½ tsp turmeric
- 1 tsp cornflour
- 1 tbsp white wine vinegar
- vegetable oil, to fry
- plain yoghurt, to garnish

1 Mix the flour with the spices and salt in a bowl. Add 150ml/¼ pint water and mix to a smooth paste. Leave to rest for 30 minutes.

2 Peel and dice the carrots, potatoes and onions. Chop 3 tablespoons of parsley. Once the flour paste has rested, mix in the vegetables and parsley.

3 Meanwhile, for the chutney, peel and dice the onion. Peel and dice the flesh from the mango. Wash, de-seed and finely chop the chillies. Wash your hands thoroughly.

Step 3

4 Heat the ghee or oil in a pan. Add the onion and cook until soft but not brown. Add the stock, sugar, mango, chillies and turmeric. Simmer the mixture for 15 minutes. Mix the cornflour with 1 tablespoon of water and add to the pan. Cook until mixture thickens and then add the vinegar. Leave to cool.

Step 4

5 Heat 1cm/½in of oil in a frying pan. Drop spoonfuls of the vegetable mixture into it, flattening them with a metal spatula. Fry for 20 minutes, or until golden brown and the vegetables are soft. Drain the pakoras on kitchen paper and serve hot with the chutney, garnished with parsley and yoghurt.

Step 5

Preparation: **30** Min Resting: **30** Min
Cooking: **35** Min
Per Pakora: 57 kcal/240 kJ;
2g protein; 2g fat; 9g carbohydrate

TYPICALLY INDIAN

In a land where water is scarce, women travel miles to fetch the precious liquid. Medieval kings used to house underground springs in stepwells. Built like a spiral staircase, the stepwell whirlpooled down into the depths of the earth to reach the cool refreshing stream.

COOKING TIPS

Gram flour is made from ground chick-peas. Substitute with half and half wholemeal flour and finely ground cornmeal • You can add chopped cauliflower, peppers and mushrooms to the pakoras • To make your own ghee, gently heat butter until the milk solids sink to the bottom. Pour off and use the fat on top.

SERVING TIP

Serve with wedges of lemon or lime, chapattis, fresh coriander and a cooling yoghurt dip.

Offer an ice-cold beer or lassi — an Indian yoghurt drink served sweet or salted.

SERVING TIP Serve with a salad of grated carrot sprinkled with toasted sesame seeds and lemon juice.

Offer a blend of orange and mango juices, maybe laced with a dash of vodka.

ℒAMB-FILLED CHAPATTIS

INDIA

Stun your guests with these Indian pitta bread equivalents. All you do is puff up the flatbreads on a griddle pan, fill them with seasoned lamb and peppers and top with a spicy yoghurt sauce.

INGREDIENTS

(Makes 20 chapattis)

- 200g/7oz wholemeal plain flour
- 100g/4oz plain flour
- 1 tbsp salt
- 2 tsp groundnut oil

FOR THE FILLING

- 1 bunch spring onions
- 1 red and 1 green pepper
- 400g/14oz lean lamb (boned leg meat)
- 1 tbsp ghee
- salt and black pepper
- 1 tbsp garam masala

FOR THE SAUCE

- 3 cloves garlic
- 4cm/1¾in fresh root ginger
- 350g/12oz natural yoghurt
- 1 tbsp medium curry powder

INGREDIENTS TIP

Ghee is sold in tins in most large supermarkets. You can substitute vegetable oil.

1 Mix the flours in a bowl with the salt and oil. Add 200ml/7fl oz of water and knead the mixture to form a soft dough. Leave to rest for 2 hours in a cool place.

2 For the filling, wash the spring onions. Wash and de-seed the peppers. Cut the onions and peppers into thin strips. Dice the lamb finely. Warm the ghee in a pan and brown the meat. Add the vegetables and cook for a further 2 minutes. Season with salt, pepper and garam masala.

3 For the sauce, peel and crush or finely chop the garlic and ginger. Mix them with the yoghurt and curry powder.

4 Divide the dough into 20 equal portions. Roll each one out into a 10cm/4in circle. Heat a heavy-based frying pan until very hot.

5 Cook the chapattis in batches for 30–60 seconds on each side, or until brown flecks appear and they puff up slightly. Serve the hot chapattis with the lamb filling. Spoon over the yoghurt sauce.

Step 1

Step 2

Step 5

Preparation: **55** Min Resting: **2** Hours
Cooking: **5–10** Min
Per Chapatti: 108 kcal/455 kJ;
7g protein; 3g fat; 13g carbohydrate

TYPICALLY WEST BENGAL

Calcutta is a stronghold of Hindu religion and the spring festival of *Holi* is celebrated with gusto. In honour of the mischievous god Vishna, revellers sprinkle each other with coloured water and powder as bright as the myriad of spices used in Indian cooking.

ℐEAFOOD TEMPURA

JAPAN

This Japanese classic consists of juicy battered scallops, prawns and broccoli with a horseradish-flavoured dip. The morsels make exotic bites to hand round, or to serve as a starter.

INGREDIENTS
(Serves 4)

- 225g/8oz broccoli florets
- 225g/8oz scallops
- 225g/8oz uncooked tiger prawns
- vegetable oil, to deep-fry

FOR THE BATTER
- 100g/4oz plain flour
- ½ tsp ground coriander
- ½ tsp ground cumin
- 1 egg
- 1 tbsp sunflower oil
- 150ml/¼ pint beer
- salt and black pepper

FOR THE DIP
- 5 tbsp mayonnaise
- 3 tbsp horseradish sauce

INGREDIENTS TIP
Use fresh scallops, on the shell if possible, so that you can be sure they are not frozen. Ask the fishmonger to prepare them for you. Cook the same day.

1 Blanch the broccoli florets in a pan of boiling water for 1 minute. Drain and rinse under cold running water. Pat dry with kitchen paper. Set aside with the scallops and tiger prawns.

2 For the batter, put all batter ingredients into a food processor or blender and mix until smooth. Transfer to a bowl.

Step 1

3 Heat the vegetable oil in a deep-fat fryer to 180°C/350°F, or pour 2.5cm/1in oil into a wok or frying pan and heat until a cube of white bread turns brown in 1 minute. Dip the broccoli florets, scallops and prawns into the batter, shaking off the excess.

Step 3

4 Fry the broccoli florets, scallops and prawns in batches of 5–6 pieces for 2–3 minutes, or until the batter turns golden brown. Drain on kitchen paper. Repeat with the remaining ingredients.

5 Meanwhile, for the dip, mix together the mayonnaise and horseradish sauce. Season to taste. Spoon the dip into a small bowl. Serve the tempura with the dip.

Step 4

Preparation: **20 Min**
Cooking: **10–15 Min**
Per Serving: 667 kcal/2769 kJ;
28g protein; 51g fat; 24g carbohydrate

TYPICALLY JAPANESE
Prawns figure prominently in many Japanese recipes, including New Year's soup. This first meal of the year, called *ozoni*, means simmered allsorts. Tokyo shuts down from 1st–4th January as everyone returns to their family home for the traditional feast.

COOKING TIP

If the fishmonger does not prepare the shellfish for you, take the shell off the prawns, leaving the tail, and remove the dark vein along the back. Cut the small strip of muscle from the white part of the scallop and discard. Remove the white meat and coral from the shell and slice in half if large. Rinse in water and dry.

SERVING TIP

Follow with a selection of sushi: rice spread with horseradish and fish or vegetables, with soy sauce.

These crunchy snacks go well with a dry white wine, such as a Muscadet from the Loire in France.

3 WAYS WITH CHEESE TARTLETS

Creamy and tasty, cheese is always a popular choice at a buffet table. Serve these shortcrust pastry tartlets at any time of day as a starter, main course or even a savoury after the dessert.

BASIC TARTLET PASTRY

Preparation: **25** Min   Chilling: **45** Min

(MAKES 16 TARTLETS)
- 125g/4½oz plain flour
- pinch of salt
- 60g/2½oz cold butter

1 Mix flour and salt. Rub in the butter and gradually add enough cold water to form a soft dough. Wrap in cling film; chill for 45 minutes.

2 Preheat the oven to 180°C/350°F/Gas 4. Divide the dough into 16 portions. Roll each into a circle and press into a greased 5cm/2in fluted flan tin. Fill with one of these recipes.

CHEESE AND BEEF TARTLETS

Preparation: **15** Min   Cooking: **25** Min

SWITZERLAND

- 50g/2oz Bündnerfleisch air-dried beef or salami
- 100g/4oz Emmental cheese
- 1 large egg
- 125ml/4fl oz double cream
- salt and pepper
- ground nutmeg

3 Finely dice the meat and cheese. Divide them equally between the tartlet cases.

4 Whisk the egg with the cream. Season with salt, pepper and nutmeg. Pour a little of the mixture into each of the tartlet cases.

5 Bake the tartlets in the preheated oven for 25 minutes, or until golden brown.

CHEESE TARTLETS WITH PRAWNS

Preparation: **15** Min   Cooking: **25** Min

DENMARK

- 75g/3oz Danish Danbo, or other medium-hard cheese, e.g. Gruyère
- 75g/3oz peeled, cooked prawns
- 1 large egg
- 125ml/4fl oz milk
- fresh dill or chives
- salt and black pepper

3 Finely dice the cheese. Divide it equally between the tartlet cases, together with the prawns.

4 Whisk the egg and milk together. Chop 2 tablespoons of dill and add. Season mixture with salt and freshly ground black pepper.

5 Pour a small amount of the egg mixture into each tartlet case. Bake in the preheated oven for 25 minutes, or until golden brown.

CHEESE TARTLETS WITH SPINACH

Preparation: **15** Min   Cooking: **25** Min

TURKEY

- 125g/4½oz fresh spinach
- 1 clove garlic
- 2 shallots
- 1 tbsp olive oil
- 100g/4oz feta cheese
- 1 large egg
- 125ml/4fl oz milk
- salt and black pepper

3 Wash and chop the spinach. Crush the garlic. Dice the shallots. Heat the oil in a pan. Add garlic and shallots.

4 Cook shallots and garlic for 5 minutes, or until soft. Add the spinach. Cook for 2–3 minutes, or until the spinach has wilted.

5 Off the heat, crumble the cheese into the spinach. Whisk the egg and milk. Season. Divide the spinach mixture between the tartlet cases. Top them up with the egg and milk. Bake the tartlets for 25 minutes, or until golden brown.

CHICKEN DRUMSTICKS WITH BLUE CHEESE DIP

USA

Satisfying to eat but simple to prepare, these succulent chicken drumsticks are marinated in chilli and garlic, then char-grilled and served with a robust blue cheese and chive dip.

INGREDIENTS

(Makes 10 drumsticks)

- 10 small chicken drumsticks
- 3 small red chillies
- 4 cloves garlic
- 5 tbsp olive oil
- salt and black pepper

FOR THE DIP

- 1 bunch chives
- 3–4 sprigs marjoram
- 300g/10½oz blue cheese
- 3 tbsp olive oil
- 300g/10½oz crème fraîche

INGREDIENTS TIP

You can use 1 teaspoon of dried marjoram instead of fresh for the dip. Choose a soft blue cheese such as Gorgonzola or Danish blue.

1 Wash and dry the chicken. Wearing rubber gloves, halve, de-seed, wash and dice the chillies. Peel and crush the garlic.

2 Mix 5 tablespoons of olive oil with the chillies, garlic, salt and pepper in a bowl. Coat each of the drumsticks in this mixture. Transfer them to a non-metallic bowl. Cover with non-PVC cling film and leave in a cool place to marinate for at least 2 hours.

3 For the dip, wash and dry the herbs, retaining a sprig of marjoram for garnish, and chop them finely. Crumble the blue cheese into a bowl. Using a fork, mash it with 3 tablespoons of olive oil until smooth. Fold in the crème fraîche and herbs. Season.

4 Preheat a griddle pan over medium-high heat and oil it lightly. Push a skewer into each drumstick. Char-grill them in 2 batches for 15–25 minutes, turning once, until golden brown on both sides. Insert a knife into the chicken to check it is cooked through — the juices should run clear. Serve the hot drumsticks with the dip, garnished with marjoram.

Step 2

Step 3

Step 4

Preparation: **30** Min
Marinating: **2** Hours
Cooking: **30–50** Min
Per Drumstick: 364 kcal/1514 kJ;
23g protein; 30g fat; 2g carbohydrate

TYPICALLY MID-WEST
In the land of cowboys — states such as Kansas, Montana, Oklahoma, South Dakota and Wyoming — hungry ranchers tuck into enormous platefuls of meat, traditionally seared over the camp fire. Such dishes readily adapt to the barbecue and outdoor parties.

COOKING TIPS

If you do not own a griddle pan, which gives attractive seared lines on the meat, grill the drumsticks for 15-25 minutes or bake them in an oven preheated to 200°C/400°F/Gas 6 for 25-30 minutes. You can also barbecue them • If liked, prepare the drumsticks the day before and refrigerate in the marinade overnight.

SERVING TIP

Serve with tortilla chips baked with melted cheese, chillies and fried onion rings.

Serve with an ice-cold lager or a 'rattlesnake' cocktail of whiskey, lemon juice and sugar syrup.

CALIFORNIAN CRABCAKES

USA

These light fishcakes from sunny California will brighten up any occasion. The crabmeat is carefully flavoured with parsley, mustard and cayenne to be tasty but not too hot.

INGREDIENTS
(Makes 10 crabcakes)

- ½ bunch flat-leaf parsley
- 2 shallots
- 1 egg
- 2 tbsp mayonnaise
- ½ tsp mustard powder
- salt
- pinch of cayenne pepper
- 75g/3oz white bread
- 75ml/2½fl oz milk
- 350g/12oz crabmeat
- 2 pink grapefruit
- sunflower oil, to fry

INGREDIENTS TIP
It is best to use the cans of crabmeat in brine that are available in supermarkets for this recipe. They consist of just white crabmeat; remove the paper and drain the meat before use.

1 Wash, dry and finely chop the parsley, reserving a few sprigs for the garnish. Peel and finely dice the shallots. Mix both with the egg, mayonnaise, mustard powder, salt and cayenne pepper.

2 Cut the bread into cubes and place in a bowl. Pour on the milk and allow to soak. Flake the crabmeat into another bowl, then mix with the bread and parsley mixture.

Step 2

3 Divide the crab mixture into 10 portions. Using your hands, shape them into round, flat cakes. Chill for 1 hour in the fridge.

4 Meanwhile, peel the grapefruits. Remove the segments by slicing down both sides of the white membranes to the core. Once all the segments are removed, squeeze out the juice from the remaining membrane and core into a small bowl.

Step 3

5 Heat a thin layer of oil in a deep frying pan. Fry the crabcakes in 2 batches for 10 minutes each side, or until they are golden brown on both sides. Serve hot or cold sprinkled with grapefruit juice and garnished with the segments and a sprig of parsley.

Step 4

Preparation: **30** Min Chilling: **1** Hour
Cooking: **40** Min
Per Crabcake: 152 kcal/633 kJ;
8g protein; 10g fat; 7g carbohydrate

TYPICALLY CALIFORNIAN
The Dungeness crab variety is native to the Pacific coast of the USA and is a highly prized delicacy in California. Its texture is firm and its taste sweet, with a large proportion of white to brown meat. At 20cm/8in across, it is a large crab, so there is plenty to tuck into.

COOKING TIPS

Try making these cakes with tuna, using the same
quantity as the crabmeat, or with a mixture of the
two. Use canned tuna in brine rather than oil • For a
lower-fat option, grill instead of frying the crabcakes.
Place them under a hot grill for 10 minutes each side.

SERVING TIP

Offer a Caesar salad with the crabcakes, or crudité strips of sweet
pepper, spring onion and chicory.

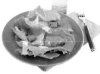

Choose a Californian Chardonnay white wine to
complement the fresh flavours in these fishcakes.

CRUNCHY POTATO SKINS

USA

Baked potato skins, filled with peppers, tomatoes and onion and topped with cheese, make a great Tex-mex party snack. A garnish of lime and spring onion adds the final touch.

INGREDIENTS
(Serves 8)

- 4 large baking potatoes
- 4 tbsp vegetable oil
- 175g/6oz Monteray Jack or Cheddar cheese
- 3 spring onions
- 2 tomatoes
- 2 jalapeño peppers
- 1 tsp paprika

INGREDIENTS TIP
Jalapeño peppers are small, hot green chillies. You can buy them fresh or canned in brine, in which case you need to drain them. Take care when de-seeding fresh jalapeños because the seeds and veins are extremely hot.

1 Preheat the oven to 200°C/400°F/Gas 6. Scrub the potatoes. Thread them onto 2 long metal skewers. Put on a baking sheet and bake for 1 hour, or until tender when pierced with a knife.

2 Increase the oven temperature to 220°C/425°F/Gas 7. Remove the skewers. Cut the potatoes in half lengthways and scoop out the flesh, leaving a 3mm/⅛in thick shell.

3 Brush the potato skins with the vegetable oil. Put them on the baking sheet and return to the oven. Bake for 25 minutes.

4 Meanwhile, grate cheese. Slice the spring onions. Chop tomatoes. Wearing rubber gloves, drain peppers, if necessary, and slice.

5 Arrange the potato skins on an ovenproof tray or dish. Scatter over half of the cheese. Add the onions, tomatoes and jalapeño peppers. Top with the remaining cheese and sprinkle with paprika.

6 Return the potato skins to the oven. Bake for a further 5 minutes, or until the cheese is melted and bubbling. Transfer to warmed plates and serve immediately.

Step 1

Step 2

Step 5

Preparation: **10 Min**
Cooking: 1½ Hours
Per Serving: 221 kcal/922 kJ;
8g protein; 13g fat; 18g carbohydrate

TYPICALLY AMERICAN
Enthusiasm for American football sweeps the USA and Superbowl parties are hugely popular. Groups of spectators tuck into platefuls of finger food while cheering on their team — just watching the pace of play is enough to work up a ravenous appetite.

COOKING TIP

Use the scooped-out potato flesh in other recipes or simply for mashed potato. Alternatively, mash, then pipe into swirls on a baking sheet and freeze for up to 1 month. Defrost for 2 hours at room temperature, then bake on the sheet for 20 minutes, until golden.

SERVING TIP

Serve with Texas hounds: hot dogs in long buns scattered with chillies.

Red wine goes well with these snacks. Try a Bardolino from northern Italy.

SERVING TIP Serve in a soft tortilla with salad, or with tortilla chips and carrot, pepper and celery strips.

Try a Mexican Petite Sirah red wine with this dip. Its mellow flavour goes well with the spicy chilli.

$\mathscr{G}$UACAMOLE PARTY DIP

INGREDIENTS
(Serves 8)

- 6 cloves garlic
- 2 red chillies
- 4 tomatoes⁻
- 2 limes
- 3 avocados
- salt and black pepper
- pinch of paprika
- 1 spring onion, to garnish
- 200g/7oz tortilla chips, to serve

INGREDIENTS TIP
The avocados need to be really soft and ripe to make this dip. Buy them a few days beforehand and leave them by a window to ripen. They are ready to use when the skin near the stalk yields slightly when pressed.

This fiery dip is typical of Mexican cuisine, and fun to eat at a party. A simple blend of ripe avocados and tomatoes, spiced up with chilli and garlic, is always a popular choice with guests.

1 Peel and roughly chop the garlic. Wearing rubber gloves, remove the stalk and seeds from the chillies and slice the flesh.

2 Reserve 1 tomato for the garnish. Cut a cross in 3 tomato skins and plunge them in a bowl of boiling water for 1 minute. Drain, then peel and chop tomatoes roughly.

Step 2

3 Place the garlic and chillies in a food processor. Squeeze the juice from the limes and add. Blend for a few minutes until finely chopped. Cut the avocados in half lengthways and twist apart.

Step 3

4 Remove the stone from the avocados. Scoop out the flesh and add it to the food processor. Blend the mixture until it is smooth. Alternatively, mash with a fork. Mix in the tomatoes. Season with salt, black pepper and paprika.

5 Put the guacamole into small serving dishes. Finely chop the reserved tomato and spring onion. Sprinkle over the guacamole. Serve with tortilla chips.

Step 4

Preparation: **20** Min
Per Serving: 121 kcal/499 kJ;
2g protein; 11g fat; 3g carbohydrate

TYPICALLY MEXICAN
Famous for its pyramids, Mexico also has a fine gastronomic tradition based on locally grown fruit and vegetables. Avocados are cultivated, but the prickly pear grows wild. This drought-resistant cactus has an edible fruit once you get past the tough thorny skin.

MEAT-FILLED EMPANADAS

PERU

In authentic Peruvian style, these crisp little pastries have an exotically spiced meat filling, flavoured with cumin, olives and hard-boiled eggs. They are delicious served hot or cold.

INGREDIENTS

(Makes 16 empanadas)

- 250g/9oz plain flour
- salt and black pepper
- 100g/4oz butter

FOR THE FILLING

- 1 onion
- 1 tbsp olive oil
- 3 eggs
- 40g/1½oz stoned green olives
- 300g/10½oz lean beef
- large pinch of chilli powder
- 1 tsp ground cumin
- 3 tbsp raisins
- tomato wedges, to garnish

INGREDIENTS TIP
Use any cut of beef for this recipe, such as topside, rump, sirloin or silverside. To save time, you can buy ready-minced beef.

1 Mix flour, 1 teaspoon of salt, the butter and 6–8 tablespoons of water to a soft dough. Cover with cling film. Chill for 1 hour.

2 For the filling, peel and dice onion. Put in a pan with 125ml/4fl oz of water and the oil. Leave to simmer until water evaporates.

3 Meanwhile, simmer 2 eggs for 9 minutes until hard. Peel and chop the eggs. Chop olives. Dice beef and add it to the onions. Cook until the meat is brown. Season with salt, pepper, chilli powder to taste and cumin. Put mixture into a bowl and add olives, hard-boiled eggs and raisins. Cool.

Step 3

4 Preheat the oven to 200°C/400°F/Gas 6. Line a baking tray with baking paper. Roll out the pastry. Cut out sixteen 11.5cm/4½in circles. Place a spoonful of filling on each circle. Fold the pastry in half over the filling. Pinch the edges together with your fingers. Place the pastries on the baking tray.

Step 4

5 Beat the remaining egg and brush over the pastries. Bake the empanadas for 25 minutes, or until golden brown. Serve garnished with tomato wedges.

Step 5

Preparation: 45 Min Chilling: 1 Hour
Cooking: 25 Min
Per Empanada: 165 kcal/690 kJ;
7g protein; 9g fat; 16g carbohydrate

TYPICALLY PERUVIAN
Peruvians of all ages enjoy their food, and mix Inca and Spanish traditions in unusual combinations. Yellow food — whether eggs, spices, corn-on-the-cob or potatoes — often predominates, possibly because the Incas worshipped the sun.

COOKING TIPS

You can make the pastry in an electric mixer or food processor rather than by hand • Once cooked, the empanadas can be frozen for a month. To serve, thaw completely, then reheat in an oven preheated to 180°C/350°F/Gas 4 for 15 minutes.

SERVING TIP

Serve with grilled fish kebabs and a spicy tomato and chilli relish, garnished with slices of lemon.

A smooth red wine from the Estramadura region of Portugal would be ideal.

DICTIONARY OF TERMS

Every country has its own ideas for nibbles to eat at a party. Find out more about the ingredients that go to make them up, and pick up some tips on technique and presentation.

Caraway seeds belong to the parsley family and have a taste of aniseed and chervil. They are used in German, Austrian, Hungarian and Scandinavian cooking to flavour sweet cakes and liqueurs as well as goulash, cheese, sausages and sauerkraut.

Crostini means 'little crusts' in Italian. They are pieces of bread fried or toasted with a savoury topping such as olive or mushroom pâté or chopped, fried tomatoes. In Italy they are eaten before the pasta course.

Dill is a herb related to fennel and has a distinctive flavour with a faint aniseed overtone. It enhances fish, especially salmon, eggs, potatoes, chicken, soups and cucumber and makes a good flavouring for salad dressing or mayonnaise. Add it at the last minute as intense cooking spoils the taste.

Empanada means 'baked in pastry' in Spanish and it is popular in Spain and parts of South America. Like Cornish pasties, empanadas are turnovers with a pastry crust and usually have a meat and vegetable filling, but can be filled with fruit for dessert. For party nibbles, you could make them ravioli-sized, called empanaditas or, for a centrepiece at a meal, create a family-sized empanada gallega.

Garam masala is a blend of up to 12 dry-roasted, ground spices, including black pepper, chillies, cardamom, cinnamon, cloves, coriander, cumin, fennel, mace and nutmeg. Garam means warm in India, and the taste and aroma warms the palate and mood. Buy in small quantities and keep in a cool dry place for 6 months.

Gorgonzola comes from a small village of the same name near Milan and is one of the world's great cows' milk cheeses. It is semi-soft and creamy in colour and texture with delicate green veining. Traditionally eaten with a pear for pudding, it also adds piquant flavour to savoury dishes.

DISPLAYING PARTY SNACKS

Your guests will get as much pleasure from seeing an appetizing plate of snacks as from eating them.

AMOUNT
Be generous if nibbles are the only food you are providing. But avoid upstaging later dishes if you are providing dinner — in this case the aim of party snacks is to whet, not fulfil, your guests' appetites.

COLOUR
Contrasting colours look striking, especially for vegetables, so try carrots or radishes next to broccoli florets, beside cherry tomatoes or yellow pepper strips, then celery or spring onions.

PATTERNS
Party snacks work well laid out in rows — and continue to look good when the plateful is half-eaten.

GARNISHES
Let your creativity run riot — as well as chopped herbs, toasted almonds and tiny croûtons, try edible flowers, carrot curls made with a potato peeler and spring onion flowers.

62

Gram flour, also called besan flour or chick-pea flour, is made from ground chick-peas. This golden flour is much used in Asian and Arabic dishes, such as pakoras and onion bhajis. You can buy it in Middle and Far East food stores. Half wholemeal flour and half fine cornmeal makes a substitute in colour and texture, although the flavour is different.

Gruyère cheese is made from cows' milk in the valley of the same name in Switzerland. It is also produced in France. It is sweet and nutty and can be eaten fresh or matured for up to 10 months. It works well in cooking, is the best cheese for a Swiss fondue and is delicious eaten on its own.

Pretzels are a cross between savoury biscuits and bread, shaped like a loose knot that owes its form to the obscure origins of the pastry in sun-worship. They can be crisp or soft.

Sambal Oelek is a classic hot chilli sauce from Indonesia, often served as a condiment. You can buy it in larger supermarkets and Asian food stores.

Skewers are used to hold and cook cubes of meat and vegetables. The resulting dish is known as kebabs in Turkish and Middle Eastern cooking and brochettes in France. The meat is usually marinated first to make it tender and tasty. Skewers can be metal or wooden, in which case soak them in cold water for 20 minutes before grilling to stop them burning in the heat.

Tempura is a Japanese speciality. Pieces of fish or vegetables dipped in batter are deep-fried and served with soy sauce. Ideal for eating standing up at a party, it can also be a festive first course.

FRYING FOR FLAVOUR AND TEXTURE

At their best, fried bites are crisp and dry on the outside and succulent inside with the taste of the ingredients enhanced.

WHICH OIL?
Most party foods are best fried in oil with relatively little flavour, such as sunflower, peanut, groundnut or safflower oil. Vegetable oil can also be used. These oils also withstand prolonged heat better than olive oil and butter.

CRISP NOT SOGGY
Preheat the oil so that the food immediately forms a crisp coat rather than absorbing fat. Do not use a lid, or the food will steam rather than fry. Fry a little at a time, so the oil does not cool down. Serve as soon as possible after frying.

DRY-FRYING
A method that brings out the flavour of spices, seeds and nuts. Heat a heavy-based frying pan on high. Toss in the food, shaking the pan from time to time. Once you can smell the food, turn out onto a cold plate.

DEEP-FRYING IN SAFETY
• *If you are buying an electric deep-fryer, choose one with an automatic cut-off facility.*
• *Alternatively, use a deep, heavy saucepan and a fine-meshed wire basket. Make sure that the pan has a close-fitting lid so you can cut off the oxygen supply if it catches fire.*
• *Heat the oil to no more than 180°C/350°F — a cube of bread should take 1 minute to brown.*
• *Fill deep-fryers with no more than a third oil.*

INDEX

Acknowledgements

Picture Credits
All cover and recipe pictures:
Meister Verlag/International Masters Publisher B.V.
Klaus Arras, Michael Brauner, Food Photography Eising, Dorothee Godert,
Neil Mersh, Pete Myers, Manuel Schnell, Philip Wilkins
Agency pictures:
Pictures for the Typically sections: Britstock-IFA: Haga, pages 41, 47;
Mothes, page 56; Kielty: page 36; Rock: page 54; Travel Ink:
Swainson, page 25; Marsden, page 38

Measuring Ingredients
Tsp - teaspoon, Tbsp - tablespoon
Teaspoons and tablespoons are level and measured using standard
measuring spoons.
Follow either metric or imperial measurements and don't mix the two.

© International Masters Publishers BV/
International Masters Publishers Ltd MCMXCVIII
Reproduced by Mullis Morgan, London, UK
Printed in Verona, Italy by Mondadori